The Gospel of the Egyptians

Mystical Teachings of the Eternal Light

A Modern Translation

Adapted for the Contemporary Reader

**Anonymous
(Gnostic Tradition)**

Translated by Tim Zengerink

© **Copyright 2025**
All rights reserved.

It is not legal to reproduce, duplicate, or transmit any part of this document in either electronic means or in printed format. Recording of this publication is strictly prohibited and any storage of this document is not allowed unless with written permission from the publisher except for the use of brief quotations in a book review.

This book contains works of fiction. Any resemblance to persons living or dead, or places, events, or locations is purely coincidental.

Table Of Contents

Preface - Message to the Reader 1

Introduction 5

Gospel of The Egyptians 10

Thank You for Reading 25

Preface - Message to the Reader

What If You Could Help Rebuild the Greatest Library in Human History?

Thousands of years ago, the Library of Alexandria stood as the crown jewel of human achievement — a sanctuary where the collected wisdom of every known civilization was gathered, preserved, and shared freely.

And then, it was lost.

Through fire, conquest, and the slow erosion of time, humanity lost not just books — but ideas, dreams, discoveries, and stories that could have changed the world forever.

Today, the Library of Alexandria lives again — and you are invited to be a part of its restoration.

Our mission is simple yet profound:

To rebuild the greatest library the world has ever known, and to translate all timeless works into every language and dialect, so that no seeker of knowledge is ever left behind again.

By joining our movement to rebuild the modern Library of Alexandria, you become part of an unprecedented mission:

- **Unlimited Access to the Greatest Audiobooks & eBooks Ever Written:**

    Instantly explore thousands of legendary works—Plato, Shakespeare, Jane Austen, Leo Tolstoy, and countless more. All instantly available to read or listen, placing a complete literary universe at your fingertips.

- **Beautiful Paperback & Deluxe Editions at Printing Cost**

    Own any title as an elegant paperback, deluxe hardcover, or stunning collectible boxset—offered to you at true printing cost, delivered straight to your door. Build your personal Library of Alexandria, crafted for beauty, built for durability, and worthy of proud display.

- **Fresh Translations for Modern Readers—in Every Language & Dialect**

    Enjoy timeless masterpieces reimagined in clear, contemporary language—no more outdated phrases or obscure references. Alongside the original versions, we're tirelessly translating these classics into every language and dialect imaginable, ensuring accessibility and understanding across cultures and generations.

- **Join a Global Renaissance of Literature & Knowledge**

   You directly support expanding our library, publishing deluxe editions at true cost, translating works into all global languages, and bringing humanity's greatest stories to people everywhere. By joining today, you're not just preserving a legacy of masterpieces; you set in motion a powerful wave of literary accessibility.

Become a Torchbearer of Knowledge.

Join us for free now at **LibraryofAlexandria.com**

Together, we will ensure that the light of human wisdom never fades again.

With gratitude and a shared love of knowledge,

The Modern Library of Alexandria Team

Visit:

www.libraryofalexandria.com

Or scan the code below:

Introduction

The Eternal Light and the Sacred Origin of Humanity

The Gospel of the Egyptians, also known as The Holy Book of the Great Invisible Spirit, is one of the most cryptic, poetic, and spiritually powerful works of early Gnostic literature. Emerging from a mystical strain of early Christianity, it conveys a vision of reality unlike anything found in the canonical gospels. Here, instead of a linear biography of Jesus or a list of moral imperatives, we encounter an intricate cosmology—one shaped by silence, emanation, and eternal Light. It is a gospel of revelation, not narrative; of divine unfolding, not historical event. In this work, divine wisdom is not just taught—it is revealed as the eternal presence that guides humanity out of darkness and into spiritual freedom.

This ancient text opens with praise to the Great Invisible Spirit—the ultimate, unbegotten Source from which all existence flows. Unlike the anthropomorphic image of God common in traditional religion, the divine here is beyond gender, beyond time, beyond comprehension. It is pure Light, beyond thought or name, yet it expresses itself through emanations—holy beings who unfold from the source like light from a flame. These emanations, known as aeons, form the divine realm of fullness (pleroma), and their purpose is to reflect the perfection of the Source.

From this fullness emerges Barbelo, the first thought and mother of all. She is wisdom, presence, and the divine womb through which further emanations proceed. She is both the revealer and the reveled, representing the dynamic interplay of knowing and being known. Her role is central to this gospel, which portrays the divine not as a static hierarchy but as a living, breathing relationship of divine energies. The creation of the spiritual world is not a moment in time but a continuous flow of Light, of which all true being is a part.

However, in the Gnostic view, something went awry. A lower being, sometimes called Yaldabaoth or Saklas, came into existence apart from the divine harmony. Ignorant of his origin, he created the material world in darkness and pride. Believing himself to be the only god, he imposed his flawed order upon creation and trapped divine sparks within bodies of flesh. This is the Gnostic explanation for the suffering and confusion of the material world. It is not the product of a benevolent creator but of a misguided power who veils the truth.

Into this cosmos enters the voice of revelation—the savior sent from the Light. In this gospel, the savior's role is not to offer atonement through blood, but enlightenment through knowledge. He comes to awaken the divine spark within humanity, to remind us of our true home, and to offer the teachings that allow us to transcend the realm of illusion and return to the eternal Light. His teachings are not rules but riddles, not instructions but revelations—designed to dismantle the illusions of the world and prepare the soul for ascent.

The Journey of the Soul and the Power of Divine Silence

One of the most striking features of The Gospel of the Egyptians is its emphasis on the journey of the soul. The soul, in this text, is not a blank slate or a vessel of sin—it is a divine fragment, exiled in a world that does not recognize its source. The spiritual path is not one of conversion or conformity but of awakening and remembrance. The soul must travel through layers of forgetfulness, passing through realms of power and deception, to reclaim its identity as a child of the Light.

This journey is made possible through gnosis—inner knowledge. But gnosis here is not intellectual understanding; it is direct, experiential recognition of the divine presence within. It is the moment of remembering what has always been true: that the soul belongs not to the world of form and illusion, but to the realm of eternal being. This remembering is facilitated by the teachings of the savior, who guides the soul not with doctrine but with symbolic speech, sacred names, and initiatory wisdom.

The text also emphasizes the role of silence. Before creation, there was silence—not absence, but potential. From this sacred silence, the Word emerged. Silence is not empty; it is the womb of wisdom. In the Gnostic vision, silence represents the divine mystery that cannot be spoken, only experienced. It is the space between the words, the stillness behind the forms, the eternal ground from which Light arises. Those who would know the divine must learn to listen—not to the noise of the world, but to the silence that speaks within.

The use of sacred names and invocations throughout the text reflects an esoteric spiritual tradition. These names are not meant to be decoded like puzzles, but contemplated as mantras—vibrations that align the soul with divine truth. Each name reveals an aspect of the divine being and helps the soul resonate with the higher realms. For modern readers unfamiliar with this tradition, these sections may seem strange or impenetrable. But when read as part of a mystical path—as signposts rather than sentences—they become portals to deeper understanding.

This modern adaptation has been crafted with the intent to preserve the sacred rhythm, depth, and mystery of the original while presenting it in a form that speaks to contemporary spiritual seekers. Obscure terms have been gently clarified, poetic cadences retained, and symbolic language honored. The result is a version of the text that invites reflection, contemplation, and transformation.

The Gospel of the Egyptians is not a book to be read quickly or casually. It is a spiritual companion, a sacred map, a divine song. It does not explain—it reveals. It does not instruct—it invites. It is meant not to be mastered but to be entered, as one enters into mystery. As you read, let go of the need to understand everything. Let the words wash over you. Let the images stir your soul. Let the silence between the lines speak to the silence within you.

In this text, you will find echoes of ancient wisdom and glimpses of eternal truth. You will encounter the Light that knows no end, the divine mystery that holds all things, and the invitation to return—to remember—to awaken. This is the message of the gospel: that the Light is within you, that the path home is already beneath your feet, and that divine wisdom is always waiting, just beyond the veil, in the silence where the eternal speaks.

Gospel of The Egyptians

The sacred writings of the Egyptians talk about the great invisible Spirit, the Father whose name cannot be spoken. He comes from the highest perfection, shining as the purest and most eternal light. He is the Father of silence, the source of truth, and the light that never fades. He is beyond description, beyond time, and cannot be fully understood. He is the eternal Father of all, the one who created himself and exists forever.

From him came three great powers: the Father, the Mother, and the Son. They all came from the silent and incorruptible Father.

From this divine presence came Domedon Doxomedon, the eternal realm of light. In this way, the Son appeared as the fourth presence, the Mother as the fifth, and the Father as the sixth. He is beyond all power and glory, greater than anything in existence.

At this moment, the three powers—the Father, the Mother, and the Son—came together and created three realms, known as the three ogdoads. The Father brought them into being in silence and wisdom.

- The first realm belongs to the thrice-male child, containing thought, word, eternal life, will, mind,

and knowledge. This realm represents the Father, both male and female.
- The second realm is the Mother, known as the virgin Barbelon. She is a mysterious and indescribable power, existing in harmony with the Father of silence.
- The third realm is the Son, the shining crown of silence, the glory of the Father, and the strength of the Mother. From him came the seven great lights, the seven voices, and the words that complete them.

These three powers, forming the three divine realms, came from the Father's own being.

Domedon Doxomedon, the eternal realm, appeared with its throne, surrounded by powers, glories, and beings that never fade. This throne was established and marked with a name too sacred to be spoken. Hidden within a mysterious and invisible symbol, this name remains unknown.

The three powers gave praise to the great invisible Spirit, the unnameable, pure Father, and his sacred presence. They sought power from the living silence, which created glories and incorruptible beings across endless realms. The thrice-male child, filled with the greatness of silence, gave honor and asked for more divine power.

From this, the child of the great Christ, anointed by the invisible Spirit, gave praise to the Spirit and to Youel, the sacred presence. This power is beyond description, too great for words. The thrice-male child honored this greatness and sought its strength.

Then another being appeared, revealing the hidden mysteries. This being was connected to the silence and the male virgin, Youel. After this, Esephech, the child of the child, also appeared.

Thus, the divine family was complete: the Father, the Mother, the Son, and the five seals. These unshakable powers represent the great Christ, the source of all that never fades. Together, they are the powers, glories, and beings of the eternal divine fullness.

The sacred texts describe how praise was given to the unseen and mysterious Spirit, whose greatness is beyond human understanding. This Spirit remains hidden, beyond words, its glory beyond imagination. Surrounding this Spirit are countless realms, thrones, and powerful beings, all filled with divine light. Together with the Father, the Mother, the Son, and the fullness of divine power, they form the ultimate mystery.

From this divine source, Providence appeared, coming from the silence of the Spirit, carrying the Word of the Father and a brilliant light. Providence carried the five seals given by the Father and moved through the realms, establishing thrones of glory and countless angels. These angels, full of power and free from corruption, lifted their voices in eternal praise, singing together to the Father, the Mother, the Son, and the fullness of divine light, including the great Christ who came from silence.

The great Christ is known as Telmael, Telmachael, Eli Eli, Machar Machar Seth, and he represents the power of eternal life. With him are Youel, the sacred presence, and Esephech, the holder of glory, who is the child of the child and the crown of divine light. Together, they complete the five seals, part of the fullness of eternal light.

The great Word, known as the divine Autogenes, appeared along with the incorruptible Adamas. Adamas, the first man and the light of creation, was brought into existence by the unknowable Father's will. Born from pure light, Adamas was meant to correct the flaws of creation. When the great Word and Adamas came together, a new creation was formed through the power of the Word.

Adamas praised the great Spirit and the divine beings around him. He also asked for strength to help the Autogenes complete the work of the four great realms. Through this, the invisible Father's light and power would shine, and from Adamas, the great incorruptible Seth was born. Seth became the father of a holy and unchanging people, meant to carry the divine voice and silence.

From above, the power of the great light was revealed, bringing forth four great lights: Harmozel, Oroiael, Davithe, and Eleleth. Together with Seth, they formed the hidden mysteries of divine creation. Each of these lights had a companion that completed the divine order—Harmozel with Grace, Oroiael with Perception, Davithe with Understanding, and Eleleth with Wisdom.

As this divine order was established, messengers of light also appeared. Among them were Gamaliel, Gabriel, Samlo, and Abrasax, each paired with Memory, Love, Peace, and Eternal Life. These divine beings completed five groups of eight, creating a total of forty, representing the immeasurable power of the divine.

The great Word and the divine beings continued their praise, honoring the invisible Spirit and its greatness. They celebrated the fullness of creation, the unknown realms, and the incorruptible people of Seth, calling them the children of the great Father.

At that moment, all of creation trembled as the incorruptible beings were filled with awe. Three divine beings descended into the realms of those yet to be born, those who had created themselves, and those formed by creation. The greatness of the divine Christ appeared, establishing countless thrones, powers, and glories across the four realms. Everything unfolded in perfect harmony, shining with the infinite light and power of the divine Spirit.

The incorruptible, spiritual church grew stronger through the four great lights of the living Autogenes, the god of truth. They praised and sang together, giving endless glory to the Father, the Mother, the Son, and their complete divine power. The five seals, surrounded by countless hosts and rulers of the realms, were commanded to reveal themselves to those who were worthy. Amen.

The great Seth, son of the incorruptible man Adamas, gave praise to the great, invisible, unnameable, and pure Spirit. He also honored the male virgin, the threefold male child, Youel, Esephech—the holder of glory and the crown of his greatness—and the fullness of divine power. Then he asked for his descendants.

From this place, the great power of the great light, Plesithea, appeared. She was the mother of angels and lights, a glorious mother, and a virgin. She had four breasts and bore the fruit of Gomorrah like a flowing spring, with the fruit of Sodom connected to it. She appeared through the great Seth.

Seth rejoiced over this gift, given to him by the incorruptible child. He took his seed from Plesithea, the virgin with four breasts, and placed it within the fourth realm—or among the four realms—under the third great light, Davithe.

After five thousand years, the great light Eleleth said, "Let someone take control over chaos and the underworld." A cloud appeared, called Hylic Sophia, and she looked over the chaos. Her face was unique, and her form was the color of blood. The great angel Gamaliel spoke to Gabriel, the servant of the great light Oroiael, and said, "Let an angel be created to rule over chaos and the underworld."

The cloud reacted and split into two, each part holding light. A throne was placed within the cloud above. Sakla, a great angel, saw Nebruel, a demon who was with him. Together, they became the spirit of creation on earth and brought forth angels to help them. Sakla said to Nebruel, "Let there be twelve realms in this place." He then added, "By the will of Autogenes, the number seven shall be established." Sakla commanded the angels, "Go, and each of you will rule over your own world."

Each of the twelve angels set out. The first was Athoth, also known by another name. The second was Harmas, called the eye of fire. The third was Galila. The fourth was Yobel. The fifth was Adonaios, also known as Sabaoth. The sixth was Cain, whom people associate with the sun. The seventh was Abel. The eighth was Akiressina. The ninth was Yubel. The tenth was Harmupiael. The eleventh was ArchirAdonin. The twelfth was Belias. These twelve became the rulers of the underworld and chaos.

After creating the world, Sakla declared to his angels, "I am a jealous god, and nothing exists apart from me." He believed in his own power. However, a voice from above spoke, saying, "The Man exists, and so does the Son of Man." This voice came from the reflection of the divine image above, revealing the first being.

Because of this, Metanoia was born. She gained completeness and strength through the will of the Father. She created the great, incorruptible, and unshakable race of mighty men connected to Seth. Her purpose was to plant these seeds in the realms and fix the flaws in creation. Metanoia descended into the world like the image of the night, praying for the repentance of the rulers and authorities of this realm. She also prayed for the pure descendants of Adam and Seth, who shined like the sun.

The great angel Hormos then arrived to prepare, through the Holy Spirit, a sacred vessel for the lineage of Seth. This vessel would come from the corrupted world of this realm, ensuring the holy descendants of Seth would continue.

The great Seth came and planted his seed in the realms that had already been created. The number of these realms was the same as that of Sodom. Some say Sodom was the land of the great Seth, also called Gomorrah. Others believe Seth took his plant from Gomorrah and moved it to another place, which he called Sodom.

This race came into existence through Edokla. She gave birth, through the Word, to Truth and Justice, which became the foundation of the seed of eternal life. This seed remains with those who endure because they understand where they came from. This great, incorruptible race traveled through three different worlds before reaching this one.

The flood was sent as a sign of the completion of the age, coming into the world because of this race. A great fire will also come upon the earth. Grace will stay with those who belong to this race, protected by the prophets and guardians who keep their life safe. Because of this race, there will be famines and plagues. These events will happen because of the great, incorruptible race, and many temptations and false prophets will arise.

The great Seth saw how the devil plotted against his unshakable and incorruptible people. He noticed how the devil's powers and angels were confused and worked against themselves. Seeing this, Seth praised the nameless, pure Spirit, the male virgin Barbelon, the threefold male child Telmael Telmael Heli Heli Machar Machar Seth, the living power, and the male virgin Youel. He also honored Esephech, the one who holds the crown of glory, the great Doxomedonaeon, and all the powers, thrones, and divine beings mentioned before. Then, Seth asked for protection over his people.

In response, four hundred heavenly angels were sent from the great realms to watch over the people of Seth and their descendants. Leading them were the mighty Aerosiel and Selmechel. These guardians would stay until the end of this age and the final judgment of the rulers, who had been condemned by the great judges.

The great Seth was sent by the four lights according to the will of Autogenes, the divine power, and the blessing of the invisible Spirit and the five seals. He passed through three major events—the flood, the fire, and the judgment of the rulers, powers, and authorities—to save those who had lost their way. This was done through restoring the world and offering baptism in a body that Seth had prepared through a virgin. In this way, the Holy Spirit would bring forth saints through hidden signs.

This restoration reconnected the world to its original state, rejecting the false god of the thirteen realms and gathering the saints and the ineffable ones. It embraced the eternal source, the great light of the Father, and the holy baptism given through divine Providence. This baptism was higher than the heavens and was established by Jesus, the living one, whom Seth carried within him. Through Jesus, the powers of the thirteen realms were overcome, and those who followed him were strengthened with the knowledge of truth and the power of incorruptibility.

The great servant Yesseus Mazareus Yessedekeus appeared, along with the living waters and the great leaders James the Great, Theopemptos, and Isaouel. Others present included Micheus, Michar, and Mnesinous, who watched over the spring of truth, and those responsible for baptizing the living and purifying them. Sesengenpharanges also presided, alongside Micheus and Michar, who guarded the gates of the waters. Seldao and Elainos stood watch over the mountain.

The ones assigned to receive Seth's people—the incorruptible and mighty ones—were also there. Among them were the servants of the four lights: Gamaliel, Gabriel, Samblo, and Abrasax. Guardians of the sunrise, Olses, Hypneus, and Heurumaious, watched alongside rulers like Mixanther and Michanor, who ensured the chosen ones could enter eternal peace. Protectors of the souls of the elect, Akramas and

Strempsouchos, were also present, as well as the great power Heli Heli Machar Machar Seth.

The incorruptible man Poimael, along with those who are truly worthy, will take part in the baptism of the spring. They will recognize those who receive them, and they will also be recognized in return. These individuals will never experience death.

IE IEUS EO OU EO OUA!

Truly,

O Yesseus Mazareus Yessedekeus,

O living water, O child of the child, O glorious name!

Truly,

AION O ON,

IIII EEEE EEEE OOOO UUUU OOOO AAAA!

Truly,

EI AAAA OOOO,

Eternal one who sees all things!

Truly,

Translated by Tim Zengerink

A EEEEE IIII UUUUU OOOOOOO,

You who exist forever and never change!
Truly,
IEA AIO,

The one who dwells within the heart,
U AEI EIS AEI,
EI O EI, EI OS EI,

You are who you are, you are what you are!

Your great name is within me, O self-begotten, perfect one who lives inside me. I see you, the one who is visible to all. Who could ever describe you in another language? Now that I know you, I am one with the eternal. I have clothed myself in the armor of light; I have become light!

The Mother is here, her beauty shining with grace. Because of this, I lift my hands in reverence. I have been formed in the circle of the riches of light within me, which brings forth countless beings in the light, a place free from complaint or suffering. I will declare your glory with honesty, for I have come to understand you:

SOU IES IDE AEIO OIS,

O eternal one, O God of Silence!

I honor you completely. You are my resting place, O Son ES ES O E, the formless one who dwells among those without form. You lift humanity, purifying me into your life, according to your eternal name. Because of this, the sweet incense of life is within me. I have mixed it with water, following the pattern of the rulers, so that I may live with you in the peace of the saints—you who exist forever in truth.

This is the book the great Seth wrote and placed upon high mountains, untouched by the sun and beyond its reach. Since the time of the prophets, apostles, and preachers, this name has never been spoken in their hearts, nor could it be. Their ears have not heard it.

The great Seth wrote this book over 130 years, using sacred letters. He hid it in the mountain called Charaxio so that at the end of time, by the will of the divine Autogenes and the fullness of divine power, through the gift of immeasurable fatherly love, it might be revealed. This revelation is for the incorruptible, holy people of the great savior and those who dwell with them in love. It is for the great, invisible, eternal Spirit, his only-begotten Son, the eternal light, his great, incorruptible consort, the pure Sophia, the Barbelon, and the entire fullness of eternity.

Amen.

The Gospel of the Egyptians
The sacred, divine book.

May grace, wisdom, understanding, and guidance be with the one who has written it—Eugnostos the beloved, in the Spirit—in the flesh. My name is Gongessos, with my fellow beings of light in incorruptibility.

Jesus Christ, Son of God, Savior, Ichthus.

This sacred book is written by the great, invisible Spirit.

Amen.

The Holy Book of the Great Invisible Spirit.

Amen.

Thank You for Reading

Dear Reader,

We hope this timeless classic has sparked your imagination and enriched your literary journey. Now that you've turned the final page, we want to share a vision for the future of reading—one where every classic you've ever wanted to explore is at your fingertips, in a format that best suits your life.

We'd like to invite you to gain immediate, unlimited digital & audiobook access to hundreds of the most treasured literary classics ever written—along with the option to secure deluxe paperback, hardcover & box set editions at printing cost. Together, we can spark a new global literary renaissance alongside our small, independent publishing house called "The Library of Alexandria."

Thousands of years ago, the Library of Alexandria stood as a beacon of knowledge—until it was lost to history. We aim to reignite that spirit of preservation and discovery right now, in the modern age—only this time, it's accessible to all, in every language and every format.

Picture a world where every timeless classic, novel, poem, or philosophical treatise is not only available to read but also updated for today's readers—modernized, translated into any language or dialect, and ready to enjoy in any format you choose, whether that is in an eBook, audiobook, paperback, or deluxe hardcover & box set version a printing cost.

By joining our movement to rebuild the modern Library of Alexandria, you become part of an unprecedented mission to offer:

- **Unlimited Audiobook & eBook Access to the Greatest Classics of All Time**

    Instantly explore thousands of legendary works, from Plato and Shakespeare to Jane Austen and Leo Tolstoy. All are instantly ready to read or listen to, giving you a complete literary universe at your fingertips.

- **Paperback & Deluxe Editions at Printing Costs:**

    Purchase any title in a paperback, deluxe hardbound, or deluxe boxset edition at printing costs, shipped right to your doorstep. Curate your personal library of Alexandria with editions worthy of display—crafted to last, designed to captivate, and delivered straight to your door.

- **Modern translations for Contemporary Readers in all languages and dialects**

  Discover a vast selection of classics reimagined in clear, current language—no more struggling with outdated phrases or obscure references. Next to the original versions, we aim to offer translations in as many languages and dialects as possible.

  As we continue our translation efforts and add new languages, readers everywhere can connect with these works as if they were written today. By bridging linguistic divides, you're contributing to ensuring that these timeless stories become more meaningful, accessible, and inspiring for people across the globe.

- **Your Personal Library of Alexandria:**

  Over the months and years, you'll curate a unique physical archive of classics—each volume a testament to your taste, curiosity, and love of knowledge. It's not just about owning books—it's about curating a cultural legacy you'll cherish and pass down for generations to come.

- **Join a Global Literary Renaissance:**

  Your support fuels an ongoing mission: allowing us to reinvest in offering deluxe print editions (including special boxsets) at their true cost, broaden the range of available formats and translations, and extend the reach of these works to new audiences worldwide. By joining today, you're not just preserving a legacy of masterpieces; you set in motion a powerful wave of literary accessibility.

We are more than a publisher—we're a movement, and we can't do it alone. Your support lets us scale our mission, preserving and reimagining history's greatest works for tomorrow's readers.

Become a Torchbearer of knowledge.

Thank you for picking up this book and allowing us into your literary journey. As you turn the pages, know that you're part of something larger: a global effort to keep these stories alive, share their wisdom across borders and generations, and spark a true cultural revival for the modern era.

If this resonates with you—please consider taking the next step by visiting:

www.libraryofalexandria.com

With gratitude and a shared love of knowledge,

The Modern Library of Alexandria Team

Visit:

www.libraryofalexandria.com

Or scan the code below:

www.ingramcontent.com/pod-product-compliance
Lightning Source LLC
LaVergne TN
LVHW030632080426
835512LV00021B/3467